Our Puget Sound

Birds & Habitat

Including Other Washington Locations

To Gwenn,
Enjoy the birds!

Craig Johnson
Joy Johnson

ORANGE SPOT PUBLISHING

Preface

Western Washington natives, Craig and Joy both grew up spending time outdoors, sailing, hiking and camping in the beautiful Puget Sound area. This early exposure gave them an appreciation of nature and wildlife, which has persisted. With camera and binoculars in hand, they have enjoyed countless hours exploring natural areas of the Puget Sound region and elsewhere in Washington State.

Photography is a recent development in Craig's art career. From an early age, he has been a professional artist (some of his watercolor bird paintings adorn pages 2 and 3 of this book). Several years ago, he began photographing birds for fun and identification. Always hand holding the camera, rather than using a tripod, he now uses an f4-5.6, 200-400mm lens. All graphic layout in the book is Craig's handiwork as well. Writing the text was an opportunity for Joy to relive many great birding experiences and share information.

This book, their third, presents an array of birds organized by their habitat. As Craig and Joy found, colorful close-up photos of the birds can aid in identification. The bird photos are all labeled with bird name and location. All birds were photographed in Washington State, primarily in the Puget Sound region. Most of the photos are new, including several species not represented in their previous books, *Our Puget Sound Backyard Birds I & II*.

After watching birds intensely for many years and achieving a Certificate in Ornithology from the Cornell Lab of Ornithology, Craig and Joy have grown to recognize the critical importance of maintaining appropriate habitat areas for these amazing and diverse creatures to live and breed. Beyond providing human enjoyment, birds play intricate roles in the ecosystem of our planet and would be sorely missed by all if they were to disappear. With the goal of inspiring others to appreciate birds and their needs, proceeds of this book will be donated to promote wildlife preservation.

In memory of Joy's mother, Wilma Helton, and Craig's uncle, Errett Crowther

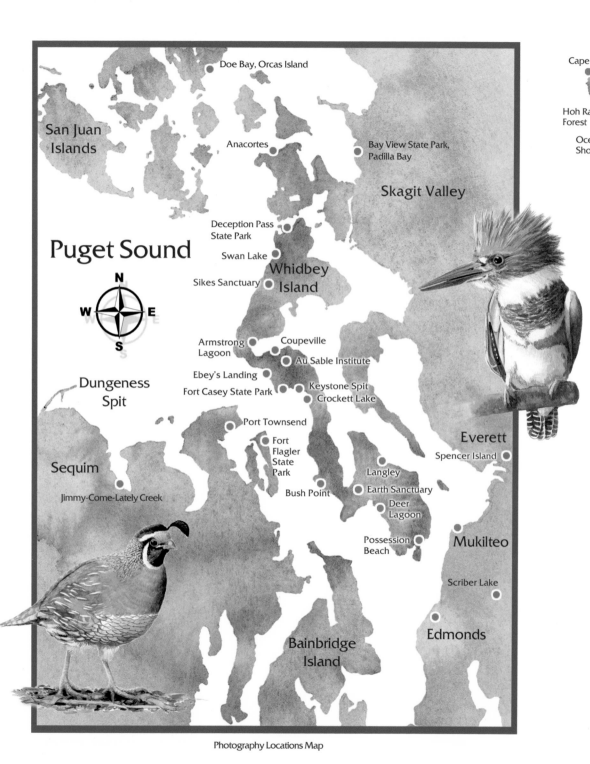

Doe Bay, Orcas Island

San Juan Islands

Anacortes

Bay View State Park, Padilla Bay

Skagit Valley

Deception Pass State Park

Puget Sound

Swan Lake

Whidbey Island

Sikes Sanctuary

Armstrong Lagoon

Coupeville

Au Sable Institute

Ebey's Landing

Fort Casey State Park

Keystone Spit
Crockett Lake

Dungeness Spit

Port Townsend

Fort Flagler State Park

Everett

Spencer Island

Sequim

Langley

Bush Point

Earth Sanctuary

Deer Lagoon

Jimmy-Come-Lately Creek

Possession Beach

Mukilteo

Scriber Lake

Edmonds

Bainbridge Island

Photography Locations Map

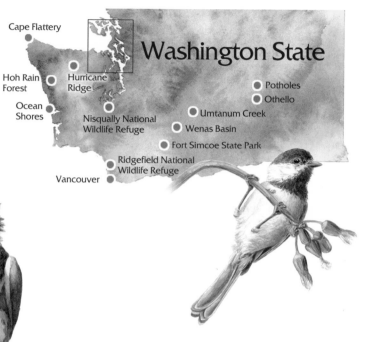

Cape Flattery

Washington State

Hoh Rain Forest

Hurricane Ridge

Potholes

Othello

Ocean Shores

Umtanum Creek

Nisqually National Wildlife Refuge

Wenas Basin

Fort Simcoe State Park

Ridgefield National Wildlife Refuge

Vancouver

Table of Contents

Woodland - Riparian

Densely wooded areas are crucial for many birds to breed and escape from predators. These birds have adapted over time to occupy particular areas within the forest, where they find shelter, nesting space and forage areas. Closer to the edge, they are more vulnerable to predation and the elements, so it is considered less desirable habitat by these species. For birdwatchers, viewing birds in the forest is challenging because they have so many places to hide, plus lighting is subdued or patchy. In order to get a good look at some of these birds, it may help to look along the edge of their habitat where lighting is better. Water is one thing that will bring birds out to the edge, therefore riparian, or river edge, habitat can be a rewarding place to look for birds.

Colorful songbirds, like these warblers, can often be found along the edges of rivers and streams. As insect eaters, they can be seen flitting about among leafy trees and shrubs. Most warblers are migratory, but the Yellow-rumped can be seen in the Puget Sound area all year.

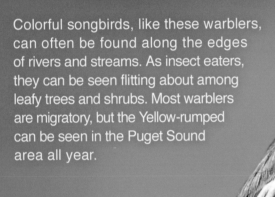

Yellow-rumped Warbler "Myrtle", male

Townsend's Warbler, male   Fort Casey State Park

Yellow-rumped Warbler "Audubon's", male   Earth Sanctuary

Scriber Lake

Yellow Warbler, male   Spencer Island

Wilson's Warbler, male   Fort Casey

Yellow-rumped Warbler, juvenile   Fort Casey State Park

5

Spencer Island

With a wide variety of habitat adaptations, warblers can be found near the ground foraging in mud, like the Common Yellowthroat, or high in the canopy, as with the Yellow Warbler. Sometimes they will be in mixed flocks, all moving about the tree branches, gleaning insects at a frenetic pace.

Orange-crowned Warbler   Fort Flagler State Park

Orange-crowned Warbler

Common Yellowthroat, male

Yellow Warbler, male   Wenas Basin

Another colorful summertime visitor is the Bullock's Oriole. The male's brilliant plumage is quite eye-catching, while the female and juvenile are much more subdued. Common in eastern Washington, they are uncommon in the Puget Sound area. Finding a breeding pair at Possession Beach was an unexpected treat. We watched the female capture insects on blackberry brambles and bring them back to an impatient fledgling.

Similar to the male Bullock's Oriole, the male Black-headed Grosbeak also has bright colors contrasting with dark and white on the wings and tail. A distinctively black head sets the grosbeak apart.

Bullock's Oriole, juvenile

Bullock's Oriole, female

Black-headed Grosbeak, male

Bullock's Oriole, male   Possession Beach

Pine Siskin   Bush Point

A serious threat to many species of songbirds is the parasitic nesting behavior of the Brown-headed Cowbird. Never building its own nest, the cowbird lays its eggs in the nests of other birds and relies on them to incubate and raise its young, often to the demise of the host bird's own offspring.

Brown-headed Cowbird, male   Fort Casey State Park

Warbling Vireo   Fort Casey State Park

Cassin's Finch, female   Wenas Basin

A flock of at least one hundred Evening
Grosbeaks foraged voraciously on
blossoming trees alongside the road,
adding to the brilliant colors of spring
in the Wenas Basin.

Evening Grosbeak, female   Wenas Basin

Evening Grosbeak, male   Wenas Basin

Cedar Waxwing, juvenile

Dozens of Cedar Waxwings descended upon the Earth Sanctuary in early summer. Sallying after flying insects kept them busy with only brief pauses to rest.

American Goldfinch, male   Bush Point

Western Tanager, female

With its bright, tropical colors, the male Western Tanager is a splendid summer visitor. Nesting in coniferous forests, these birds can sometimes be spotted gleaning vegetation or flying after insects.

Our state bird, the American Goldfinch, male, has a similarly bright yellow breeding plumage, without the red head. A common feeder bird, the goldfinch can also be seen eating thistle seeds in open fields late in the summer.

Western Tanager, male   Earth Sanctuary

Red-breasted Nuthatch, juvenile   Doe Bay

Song Sparrow, juvenile
Bush Point

House Wren, juvenile   Fort Casey State Park

Black-headed Grosbeak, juvenile   Doe Bay

Late spring is the time to look for baby birds, fresh out of the nest, learning to forage and fend for themselves. It can be tricky to identify the subdued plumages of juvenile birds, but the wider, soft cornered mouth, or gape, along with the fuzzy look about their feathers can help identify immatures.

Dark-eyed Junco, juvenile   Bush Point

Swainson's Thrush, juvenile   Bush Point

Chestnut-backed Chickadee, juvenile   Bush Point

Fluffy little puffballs, Bushtits move along through trees and shrubs in groups of up to forty after breeding season, continuously calling to one another with short, high notes. Male and female look alike, except the male has black eyes and the female's eyes are yellow.

In the fall, Bushtits and Chickadees can often be seen dangling by their feet, collecting insects and seeds from lower vegetation.

Bushtit, female   Bush Point

Black-capped Chickadee

Bushtit, male   Fort Casey State Park

When we are standing quietly near the tree line at Fort Casey State Park, tiny kinglets will sometimes come by in a small foraging flock. They flit around the branches, deftly extracting insects, seemingly all around us, calling to one another. Then, as quickly as they appeared, they fly off to another area.

Ruby-crowned Kinglet   Fort Casey State Park

Golden-crowned Kinglet   Fort Casey State Park

15

Green Heron nestling   Scriber Lake

Green Heron on nest   Scriber Lake

A generally secretive bird, Green Herons can be difficult to spot. They nest in trees or shrubs over a body of water, such as the pond at Scriber Lake, where they are also able to hunt for a meal of amphibians, small fish or aquatic insects.

Green Heron, juvenile   Deer Lagoon

Eastern Kingbird   Spencer Island

Fierce defenders of their breeding territories, Eastern Kingbirds will chase off much larger birds without hesitation. Uncommon in the west, they have been spotted at Spencer Island for several summer breeding seasons.

Male birds belting out their territorial and courtship songs in the spring can make it easier to locate them. With their focus on defending territory and attracting a mate, they tend to be more prominently displayed and less concerned about curious humans.

Marsh Wren   Spencer Island

Bewick's Wren   Possession Beach

Chipping Sparrow   Wenas Basin

Fox Sparrow   Spencer Island

Lincoln's Sparrow   Spencer Island

Some birds are particularly well camouflaged and can be challenging to discern unless they move, like the Brown Creeper. It tends to start at the base of a tree and spiral up the trunk, gobbling invertebrates from under the bark as it goes. When it reaches the top, it flies down to the base of a nearby tree and begins again.

Walking through the woods, birds are heard more often than seen. Learning their calls and songs can therefore help to identify them. Additionally, knowing that a Red Crossbill eats seeds from conifer cones and a House Wren gleans insects from lower trees, shrubs and the ground will also direct the eye to particular areas where these birds may be found.

Whidbey Island

Red Crossbill, male   Doe Bay

Ruby-crowned Kinglet   Possession Beach

House Wren
Fort Casey State Park

19

Anna's Hummingbird, female   Bush Point

Anna's Hummingbird, male   Bush Point

Tucked away below a larger abandoned nest, a female Anna's Hummingbird built her own tiny cup nest. Comprised of soft plant down woven together with spider webs, it was well camouflaged by a layer of decorative lichen around the outer edge. Two hatchlings fit snugly within the one inch diameter opening (magnified in this photo). Female hummingbirds make the nest, incubate eggs and raise young all on their own.

Anna's Hummingbird, nestlings   Sikes Sanctuary

American Robin, juvenile

Swainson's Thrush   Earth Sanctuary

American Robin, male

Robins are one of the most easily recognizable birds. Readily visible as they hunt for worms on the grass, they are a common bird throughout Washington. Their lovely song is heard prominently at dawn and dusk.

Another vociferous songster is the Swainson's Thrush, whose ascending notes can be heard in most forested areas during summer.

American Robin, female   Fort Casey State Park

Shrouded by foliage and looking so much alike, flycatchers can be difficult to discern. Different degrees of lighting can even make the same species look like a new bird. Knowing what type of environment the bird prefers can help to identify it. The Pacific-slope Flycatcher is comfortable in mixed forest habitat.

Western Wood-Pewees prefer edge habitat where they will perch on a prominent branch and "hawk" after flying insects, then return to the same perch.

Pacific-slope Flycatcher   Fort Casey State Park

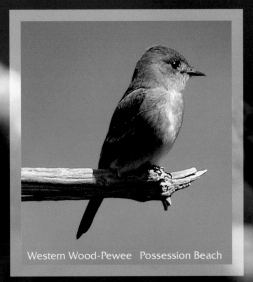

Western Wood-Pewee   Possession Beach

Pacific-slope Flycatcher   Fort Casey State Park

Striking cobalt blue plumage distinguishes the gregarious Steller's Jay, a familiar campsite visitor in the mountains who also frequents home feeders.

A fellow corvid, the Black-billed Magpie is common in eastern Washington.

Steller's Jay, juvenile   Doe Bay

Black-billed Magpie   Yakima

Steller's Jay   Kalaloch Campground

Townsend's Solitaire   Fort Flagler State Park

Winter will bring the brightly colored Varied Thrush to lower elevations, sometimes in large numbers, when there are heavy snowstorms in the mountains. Mixed in with flocks of foraging robins, this attractive thrush can be seen in lowland forests, orchards and yards.

Another bird that might make an appearance in the Puget Sound area when weather is harsh in the mountains is the Townsend's Solitaire. Swainson's Thrushes are summer breeders.

1-20-17

Swainson's Thrush   Spencer Island

Varied Thrush, male   Langley   25

A most intriguing bird with its bright red head and crazy laughing call, the Pileated Woodpecker makes even non-birders take notice.

This juvenile's crest appears to be a pink fuzz before the longer red feathers of the mature adult form.

A pair of these crow-sized woodpeckers requires more than one hundred acres of mature forest to breed and raise their young.

Pileated Woodpecker, male

Pileated Woodpecker, female   Spencer Island

Lewis's Woodpecker   Fort Simcoe

Downy Woodpecker, female – Doe Bay

These three woodpeckers all prefer riparian habitat, though they have quite different behavior patterns. Red-breasted Sapsuckers are reclusive but sometimes visible searching tree trunks for insects in environments with a stream or pond nearby.

East of the Cascade Mountains, the green and pink Lewis's Woodpecker can be found hawking after insects in isolated areas, especially those with Garry Oak stands.

The most common of the three is the Downy Woodpecker, who sometimes nests in city woodlots or parks and is a regular home feeding station visitor.

Red-breasted Sapsucker   Earth Sanctuary

Bald Eagle, juvenile
Skagit Valley

Osprey   Doe Bay

At home roosting in trees, these large
birds are certainly more difficult to spot
when perched on branches than when
flying or feeding in or near Puget Sound.

Double-crested Cormorant   Orcas Island

Turkey Vulture   Orcas Island

Crockett Lake

Great Horned Owl near American Robin

Barred Owl — Bush Point

Well hidden in the daytime forest with their cryptic coloring, these formidable hunters are sometimes exposed by other birds, such as the agitated robin above, continuously scolding and haranguing them. We have even seen a Rufous Hummingbird join in the fray.

Great Horned Owl, juvenile

Great Horned Owl   Fort Casey

29

Wetland near Deer Lagoon

Tree Swallow   Ebey's Landing

Wetland~ Agricultural

Wetlands form where water collects as run-off from higher elevations creating swamps, bogs and ponds. Estuarine environments, where freshwater meets with saltwater and they mix into brackish water with plenty of mud exposed at low tides, are another wetland habitat. Both types are necessary for the survival of many bird species. Land used for agricultural purposes often contains or adjoins wetland areas, so they are grouped together in this section.

Tree Swallow, first year female in nest box

Violet-green Swallow, male   Skagit Valley

Barn Swallow   Possession Beach

Purple Martin, male

Cliff Swallows   Nisqually N.W.R.

Swallows are known for voraciously pursuing flying insects throughout the summer months to feed their hungry offspring.

Barn Swallow, juvenile   Possession Beach wetland area

European Starling
Crockett Lake

Ebey's Landing

Ring-necked Pheasant, female   Skagit Valley

American Kestrel, female   Coupeville

Merlin, female   Ebey's Landing

Ring-necked Pheasant, male   Skagit Valley

Northern Shrike   Crockett Lake

Townsend's Solitaire   Au Sable

Western Meadowlark   Crockett Lake

Farmland and areas that were previously used for agriculture or pasturing cattle are utilized by many bird species. Merlin, Kestrel, and other birds of prey find open fields appealing for unobstructed visibility when hunting. With fence posts distributed throughout, there are many places to perch and survey the scene. Grain eating birds, like the Ring-necked Pheasant, also prefer to live near this type of environment.

Vast open areas like these can sometimes be easier places to notice unusual birds, such as the Townsend's Solitaire or Northern Shrike, who might be visiting western Washington in winter or early spring.

Canada Geese are year-long Washington residents. Groups of goslings can be seen on bodies of water throughout the state in late spring and early summer. Cropped fields are favored places for these large geese to forage.

Brant, a winter migrant to the Puget Sound, prefer to ride the waves at the edge of the surf. They rely on eelgrass as a food source, which grows in estuarine environments.

Canada Goose
Keystone Spit

Brant   Edmonds

Goslings   Ridgefield National Wildlife Refuge

Snow Goose

Greater White-fronted Goose

Tundra Swans and Snow Geese make a spectacular impression when they gather in flocks of hundreds, or even thousands, over-wintering in muddy Skagit Valley farm fields.

The Greater White-fronted Goose migrates through Washington and is also a cropland feeder.

Peregrine Falcon   Skagit Valley

Red-tailed Hawk, juvenile

Swainson's Hawk   Wenas Basin

Red-tailed Hawk

Red-tailed Hawk   Crockett Lake

Rough-legged Hawk
Skagit Valley

Agricultural fields create an open expanse that is beneficial to the hunting process of many birds of prey. Open marshland has a similar appearance and also aids these keen-visioned hunters in seeing for great distances.

Since a number of these birds nest and breed in the northern regions of Canada and Alaska during summer, winter is a good time to look for raptors perched on a telephone pole or wire, especially in the Skagit Flats, where numerous hawks and falcons come to spend the colder months.

Gyrfalcon   Skagit Valley

Peregrine Falcon   Skagit Valley

Agile flycatchers are similar in appearance, so can be tough to identify. Willow Flycatchers are common summer residents along woodland edges or low growth areas at stream outlets. A dead snag or high tree pinnacle are preferred perches for Olive-sided Flycatchers. Ash-throated Flycatchers are only seen in a small region of south-central Washington, which includes Fort Simcoe State Park.

Ash-throated Flycatcher   Fort Simcoe S.P.

Olive-sided Flycatcher

Willow Flycatcher   Possession Beach

Sage Thrasher   Possession Beach

Song Sparrow   Bush Point

At the edges of farm fields and wetlands, Song Sparrows and Brewer's Blackbirds are quite common, often popping up from brambles or shrubbery alongside the road.

Since birds fly, sometimes an unexpected visitor might appear in an area they are not typically seen, as this Sage Thrasher did on Whidbey Island. Fairly common in central Washington, this bird is not usually seen in the west.

Brewer's Blackbird, male   Ebey's Landing

Swallows and kingbirds, both insectivores, can sometimes be seen on a roadside perch, prepared to launch in pursuit of a flying insect.

White Pelicans are truly a wonder to see, gracefully flying overhead in a loose "V" formation.

American White Pelicans   Yakima

Western Kingbird   Othello

Northern Rough-winged Swallow   Fort Flagler S.P.

Chiseling a rectangular hole with their specialized dagger-like bills, this pair of Pileated Woodpeckers prepared to nest in a snag near Spencer Island. More common in dense woodland, this pair was utilizing wetland area that previously had been diked and used as farmland.

Abandoned Pileated Woodpecker nest cavities provide homes for many other species of birds and small mammals.

Below, a Tree Swallow aggressively defended its nest in a nearby tree.

Pileated Woodpecker, female and Tree Swallow

Pileated Woodpeckers, male in nest cavity, female lower left   Spencer Island

Estuarine habitats host many birds, including this lone Spotted Sandpiper busily searching for invertebrates among the pickleweed. One of the more easily recognizable sandpipers during breeding season, this species exhibits a distinctly dark spotted breast and brightly colored bill.

Spotted Sandpiper   Jimmy-Come-Lately Creek

Dowitchers probe their bills up and down into the soft mud, like a sewing machine, in search of invertebrates. Long-billed Dowitchers are more attracted to freshwater or marsh habitats, while short-billed prefer saltwater mudflats. Occasionally, they are found together.

Greater Yellowlegs may use either type of habitat, but pluck morsels out of the mud or water more sporadically than the dowitchers.

Short-billed Dowitcher, juvenile   Swan Lake

Greater Yellowlegs   Crockett Lake

Long-billed Dowitcher   Crockett Lake

Redhead, female & male   Othello

Pockets of water scattered between agricultural fields support a wealth of bird species. You can sometimes see these and other striking birds by just pulling off to the side of the road near a "watering hole" in the arid eastern Washington region near Othello.

Yellow-headed Blackbird, male   Othello

Wilson's Phalaropes, breeding

Yellow-headed Blackbird, female   Othello

Black-necked Stilt   Othello

Black-crowned Night Heron   Potholes Wildlife Area

Great Egret   Potholes Wildlife Area

Greater & Lesser Yellowlegs   Port Townsend

Gadwall, male

Green-winged Teal, male

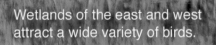

Wetlands of the east and west attract a wide variety of birds.

Northern Shoveler, male

Northern Pintail, male & female   Deer Lagoon

Ring-necked Duck, male

Great Blue Heron   Edmonds Marsh

Semipalmated Plover   Crockett Lake

The ubiquitous Killdeer is readily identifiable in a variety of habitat areas, including wetlands. Very loud cries announce its presence even when it might otherwise go unnoticed.

Crockett Lake

Belted Kingfisher, female

Common Goldeneye, female

American Wigeon, male & female

Looking out over the flood gate and channel connecting Crockett Lake to Puget Sound, a Belted Kingfisher is often poised and ready to capture unsuspecting fish as they flow through at high tide.

Many species of ducks are represented in Crockett Lake, particularly in winter.

Great Blue Heron

Great Blue Heron   Spencer Island

Marsh Wren   Edmonds Marsh

Virginia Rail   Edmonds Marsh

48

Cattails, bulrushes, and other marsh grasses create inconspicuous hiding places for birds of all sizes. Some of the more secretive of these marsh birds are the American Bittern, Pied-billed Grebe, Virginia Rail, and Marsh Wren. Their cryptic plumages allow them to disappear amongst similarly colored reeds and shadows.

Pied-billed Grebe   Ridgefield National Wildlife Refuge

American Bittern   Ridgefield National Wildlife Refuge

Natural Puget Sound shorelines often have an intermediate wetland area, as found at Possession Beach on Whidbey Island. This transition zone provides erosion control, flood protection and habitat for birds and other creatures.

Common Yellowthroat, male

Mallard, male & female

Possession Beach Park

Red-winged Blackbird, male & juvenile   Possession Beach

Rufous Hummingbird, female gathering nesting material   Possession Beach

Cinnamon Teal, male   Spencer Island

A plethora of waterfowl depend on freshwater and tidal marshland for breeding and foraging, as does the American Coot.

Hooded Merganser, male   Earth Sanctuary

Hooded Merganser, female with chicks   Earth Sanctuary

American Coot   Ridgefield National Wildlife Refuge

Spencer Island

Earth Sanctuary

Wood Duck, male   Earth Sanctuary

Precocial Wood Duck chicks are ready to walk, swim and find food about twenty four hours after hatching.

Wood Duck, female with chicks   Hoh Rain Forest

These birds of open farmland or scattered brushland blend well into their brown and gray surroundings. It is when they pop up onto a prominent branch to sing or call that they can be most readily distinguished.

Western Meadowlark

Brewer's Sparrow
Potholes

Lark Sparrow   Potholes

In winter months, the Short-eared Owl can often be seen perched on fenceposts or pilings near Crockett Lake.

Bald Eagles have made an impressive come-back since 1978 when they were listed as a threatened species and efforts were made to protect them. Having more opportunities to observe them does not take away from the awe that they inspire.

Northern Harrier, female   Skagit Valley

Merlin, female

Northern Harrier, male

Peregrine Falcon   Crockett Lake

Merlin, female

Birds of prey are generally more visible when perched on posts or flying over open fields or marsh area like the shores of Crockett Lake.

Northern Harrier, female   Crockett Lake

Northern Harrier, male
Crockett Lake

Keystone Ferry

Pigeon Guillemot   Keystone Spit

Great Blue Heron   Keystone Spit

Beach - Ocean Habitat

From the rocky shores of Puget Sound and the miles of beaches along Washington's coast, one can see birds that are water specialists offshore, waders and shorebirds at the coastline, and many other species flying overhead. Spring migration brings thousands of birds up the coast from South America to their breeding grounds in the arctic and subarctic regions of Canada and Alaska. In fall, they return. Since they stop off both ways at various "refueling" locations in Washington State, it makes this a great place to get a glimpse of these migratory visitors.

Puget Sound also has many areas that are excellent for viewing offshore birds when they come closer to land to breed during the summer months.

Red-necked Phalarope, juvenile   Keystone Spit

California Gull   Bush Point

Bonaparte's Gull with prey, non breeding

The young Bonaparte's Gull above worked hard at trying to subdue a wriggling invertebrate, retrieving it several times from the water. Finally a large, bold California Gull walked over and snatched it away.

Bonaparte's Gull, breeding   Bush Point

Black Oystercatchers   Orcas Island

Black Turnstone   Damon Point S.P.

Sanderling   Langley

Olympic Peninsula

Ruddy Turnstone

Black-bellied Plover, non-breeding

Black-bellied Plover, breeding

Greater Yellowlegs — Keystone Spit

Various types of shorebirds forage along the water's rocky edge. With their plumage blending into these surroundings, it can be tough to spot them until they move.

Least Sandpiper — Keystone Spit

Western Sandpiper — Keystone Spit

Occasionally, in addition to regular Puget Sound coastal inhabitants, like the Belted Kingfisher, we come across unexpected birds perched on driftwood along the shore. American Pipits may stop at the beach during migration or in winter. The Sage Thrasher, typically a summer resident in eastern Washington, also visited the south end of Whidbey Island in summer. Some winters will bring the Snowy Owl to more southern climes if its usual sources of prey are less abundant or when weather is particularly harsh in the north. Savannah Sparrows nest in the grasses near Keystone Spit and can be seen foraging for insects on the driftwood.

American Pipit   Keystone Spit

Belted Kingfisher, male   Coupeville

Sage Thrasher   Possession Beach

Snowy Owl   Keystone Spit

Savannah Sparrow   Keystone Spit

62

The Winter Wren is more commonly seen in forested areas, but it popped up on the beach one sunny winter afternoon.

Keystone Spit old dock

Pigeon Guillemot, juvenile – Keystone Spit

With their flashy red feet and gape, Pigeon Guillemots have an eye-catching appearance, especially in their dapper black and white breeding plumage. Year-round residents of Puget Sound and just off the ocean coast, these birds are more readily visible during the summer breeding season when they spend more time on and near the shore.

Heermann's Gull   Ebey's Landing

Eating a bit of snow is a novelty for this Glaucous-winged Gull at Keystone Spit.

Heermann's Gulls can be seen in the summer and early fall after breeding in the south. Harlequin Ducks are present on Puget Sound in the winter.

Harlequin Ducks, males and female   Keystone Spit

Glaucous-winged Gull, second year   Keystone Spit

With acute vision and controlled flight, the Osprey will hover, stoop, then plunge feet first to catch a fish.

Osprey pair on nest

Osprey with catch   Bush Point

Double-crested Cormorant

Great Blue Heron

Like the Osprey, these large birds are all fishing experts in their own fashion. Cormorants dive and swim after fish under water. Heron will stalk and stab fish with their long bills from the shallows. Eagles snatch fish from close to the surface with sharp, powerful talons or simply eat carrion washed up on the shore. Sometimes eagles will steal a hard-earned meal from an Osprey.

Bald Eagle   Keystone Spit

Surf Scoter, male   Keystone Spit

Red-necked Grebe, non breeding   Keystone Spit

Many species of waterfowl and grebes visit the coastal waters of Washington and Puget Sound in the winter. Most leave for breeding areas in the spring, some staying here just long enough to show off their fresh, colorful breeding plumage.

Red-breasted Merganser, male   Keystone Spit

Red-necked Grebe   Edmonds

Red-breasted Merganser, female   Keystone Spit

Bufflehead, male

Common Murre   Keystone Spit

Horned Grebe, non breeding

These birds all dive and swim after fish and crustaceans for food. Marinas and piers can be good places to look for water birds.

Western Grebe

Marbled Murrelet   Mukilteo

Horned Grebe   Edmonds

Closely related to puffins, Rhinoceros Auklets develop a distinctive "horn" at the base of their bright orange bill in addition to decorative plumes of white feathers that protrude from the sides of their heads during breeding season. Noted for collecting fish and clamping them securely between upper bill and tongue, these birds wait for nightfall to deliver this food to young chicks tucked safely within a cliff-side burrow. We have watched several swim just offshore for more than an hour near sunset with such a catch in their jaws, occasionally diving to evade a scavenging gull.

Rhinoceros Auklet, non breeding

Common Loon, non-breeding   Possession Beach

Diving for fish and crustaceans at the marina near Ocean Shores kept this elegant Common Loon busy for a long time, the early May sunshine accentuating its shiny, fresh breeding plumage. Occasionally it would pause and wail to another loon farther away, who would call back, apparently to maintain contact.

Pelagic Cormorant with nesting material

Sea caves - nest sites

The iridescent green and purple sheen on the Pelagic Cormorant's black feathers gave it an exotic appearance as it perched on the weatherbeaten rock at Cape Flattery. We watched several of these birds flying into the nearby seacaves with seaweed or grass used for nesting material. Surf eroded cliffs make this northwest-most point of the lower 48 states an attractive area for Pelagic Cormorants to nest.

Pelagic Cormorant   Cape Flattery

Tatoosh Island

Caspian Terns   Ocean Shores

Ocean beaches on Washington's coast offer a haven for migrating birds and local residents alike. Western Gulls can be seen at Ocean Shores all year long. Caspian Terns are found here during spring and fall migrations, before and after moving inland to breed. Mew Gulls arrive here in August to overwinter. Shorebirds can be seen foraging from mid-April to mid-May, just one refueling stop along their migration route. Many then return between July and September.

Western Gull   Ocean Shores

Western Sandpipers

Mew Gulls

Long-billed Curlew, female & Marbled Godwit, female

Short-billed Dowitcher & Marbled Godwit, female   Bill's Spit

Bill shape, overall size, and leg color can help to distinguish one shorebird from another.

Long-billed Curlew, female   Damon Point State Park

Spring, when migrating shorebirds are sporting their breeding plumage, can be a good time to make distinctions between bird species.

Dunlin   Ocean Shores

Semipalmated Plover   Ocean Shores

Sanderling   Ocean Shores

Whimbrel
Damon Point S.P.

Marbled Godwits and Western Sandpipers   Ocean Shores

Mountain - Foothills

Mountain terrain can be harsh for birds, who lack the furry coats of alpine mammals such as the mountain goat pictured, but many species continue to take advantage of this niche.

Summer is brief here, so their nesting time must be focused. When spring weather permits, migratory birds, such as the American Pipit, fly in to take advantage of the emerging summer vegetation and irruption of insects to feed their young.

Mountain Goat . Hurricane Ridge

In the parking lot at Hurricane Ridge, we watched the raven on the right scavenging along the sidewalk. After some time, what we presumed was its mate (photo taken in May) flew right up to it, squawking incessantly, feathers all ruffed up. The other gave us the most exasperated look. Then the first raven preened the other and soon both flew away to the tree line.

Allo-preening

Often recognized as a campground greeter and robber, the Gray Jay is a sociable bird, ready to seize any opportunity to find food. It is one of the few birds able to live in a hostile mountain climate year round. By coating its stored food with a sticky saliva and mucous substance it helps to ensure that the cache will not be consumed by other animals.

Hurricane Ridge

Gray Jay   Hurricane Ridge

Sooty Grouse, female   Hurricane Ridge

At one of the roadside pullouts descending from Hurricane Ridge, we were delighted to encounter a male Sooty (Blue) Grouse. He fluttered up from the shrubs below onto the shoulder of the road. After filling up his "booming sac" with air like a bagpipes, he began his hooting mating call, which was such a deep sound that it vibrated up from the ground, right through our bodies.

Performing mating call

Sooty Grouse, male   Hurricane Ridge

Mountain Chickadees are common residents in parts of the Cascade Mountains.

Both Western and Mountain Bluebirds (at the higher elevations) add brilliant color to the Wenas Basin, eastern Cascade Mountain area each summer. Efforts are being made on San Juan Island and elsewhere to help encourage Western Bluebirds to resume breeding in western Washington.

Mountain Bluebird & Bee

Clark's Nutcracker

Western Bluebird, female

Western Bluebird

Yard Environment

Creating a yard environment that encourages birds to visit can make looking out the windows much more entertaining. Whether your yard includes acres of land or an apartment patio, there are ways to invite birds to come closer. With a small investment of time and energy, the result can be mutually rewarding.

House Finch, male

House Finch, female

American Goldfinch, juvenile

Putting thistle seed out in a finch feeder during the spring and summer will attract our state bird, the brightly colored American Goldfinch.

American Goldfinch, female

American Goldfinch, male

Dark-eyed Junco

Leaving low to mid-level shrubs along the edge of the yard somewhat un-groomed will allow ground dwelling birds, like the Dark-eyed Junco, Spotted Towhee and Bewick's Wren, areas to hide and forage. Planting indigenous species will also encourage local birds to come closer.

Dark-eyed Juncos are also fond of sunflower seed and will visit birdfeeders readily, especially in fall and winter.

Bewick's Wren, juvenile

White-crowned Sparrow

Hermit Thrush

House Sparrow, male

Along with the sparrows who frequent yard settings,
it is always interesting to look for less common visitors,
such as the Hermit Thrush, who might pop out along
a forested edge or come looking for berries in the winter.

A delicate, tiny hummingbird can be the most tenacious defender of its claimed territory. We watched one Rufous male perch for most of the day on a tree branch not far from our nectar feeder, quickly ushering off all other males and some of the females who came to drink.

This type of feeder combined with a flowering hanging plant can entice these aggressive little marvels of nature to an apartment balcony during the spring migration. Sometimes the nectar feeder attracts other birds as well, like this Hairy Woodpecker!

Rufous Hummingbird, male

Hairy Woodpecker, male

Rufous Hummingbird, female

Northern Flicker, male

Northern Flicker, female

Northern Flickers are common in yard settings, both at the suet feeder and picking through the lawn for ants, one of their main food sources. Grooming a dead tree in your yard into a habitat snag could provide needed nesting and forage area for flickers and other woodpeckers, whose populations are decreasing with the reduction of forested land.

Northern Flicker, juvenile & adult male

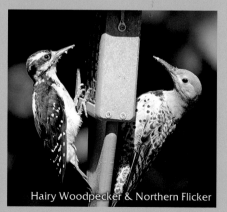
Hairy Woodpecker & Northern Flicker

Downy Woodpeckers, the smallest of the North American woodpeckers, are also comfortable in yard habitats, making use of the bird bath and suet feeder. Larger, but quite similar looking, is the Hairy Woodpecker, who often chases off the Downy.

A bird bath is an excellent way to attract birds to your yard, particularly in the dry, hot summer months. When providing a bird bath or water source, it is important to keep it clean, washing it out once a week or more, since bird illnesses, like salmonella or avian pox, can be transmitted to other birds through contaminated water.

Downy Woodpecker, male

Hairy Woodpecker, male

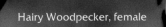
Hairy Woodpecker, female

Foraging on the ground amongst leaf litter, the Spotted Towhee prefers edges of garden beds to look for seeds and insects. Occasionally it will partake at a yard feeding station.

The Varied Thrush is a beautiful wintertime visitor. Leaving your yard free of pesticides will allow these ground feeding birds natural foods to eat.

Varied Thrush, male

California Quail, juvenile

We look forward to watching a covey of about twenty California Quail come through our yard, usually in mid-summer after the juveniles have lost their downy puff-ball look. They stay close together, with one male perched on a high rock or even our deck railing to watch for any sign of trouble. If he makes a call, they all rush for cover.

California Quail, female

California Quail, male

Pecking at the ground for scraps of seed that the other birds dropped, the pigeons and doves are our clean-up crew around the feeding station.

Band-tailed Pigeon

Rock Pigeon

The juvenile Cooper's and Sharp-shinned Hawks are brown and white with pale yellow eyes, like the Sharp-shinned Hawk pictured. As they mature, the eyes turn more orange and the feathers take on the gray-blue hue of the adult. The fully developed adults have intense red eyes and reddish-brown streaks across a white breast. The Cooper's Hawks are larger in size than Sharp-shinned. Hunting song birds that congregate around bird feeders is a common behavior for these raptors in winter.

Cooper's Hawk, adult

Cooper's Hawk, adult

Sharp-shinned Hawk, juvenile

Red-breasted Nuthatches are curious little birds with a taste for sunflower seeds, which they hide one at a time in the bark of trees. Common feeder visitors in the winter, along with Steller's Jays who favor peanuts.

Western Scrub-Jays have expanded their southwestern lowland range to the north as far as Seattle.

Western Scrub-Jay   Vancouver

Steller's Jay

Red-breasted Nuthatch, male

People seem to either love them or hate them, but crows have adapted well to urban environments and continue to thrive. Noted for their high intelligence and ability to solve problems, they are generally wary of humans though they exist easily among us.

Crows have a complex social structure with a distinct hierarchy. Breeding pairs tend to stay together and young from the previous year often remain with their parents to assist with raising new offspring, thus learning more about parenting and increasing survival rates.

The avian world is fascinating and vast, with much that humans are only beginning to study and understand. It is up to each one of us to be good stewards of the natural world, ensuring that these amazing creatures are preserved to be appreciated by future generations.

For more information on birds, contact your local Audubon Society or wild bird store.

American Crow

Index

Acknowledgments

Dr. Dennis Paulson, prolific author and educator on the subjects of birds, dragonflies and other parts of our natural world, for sharing his expertise.

Frances Wood, author of *Brushed by Feathers: A Year of Birdwatching in the West* and writer of an award-winning newspaper column about birdwatching, for her suggestions as a writer and naturalist.

Lynda Blakely, retired educator and avid birdwatcher, for her consistent encouragement and thorough proof-reading skills.

References: The Birds Of North America Online, Cornell Lab of Ornithology and the American Ornithologists Union. 2004-2005 www.bna.birds.cornell.edu
Bell, Brian H., Gregory Kennedy. 2006. Birds of Washington State. Lone Pine Publishing International, Inc. Auburn, WA.